Travis Wayne Goodsell's Buyer's Checklist

Ancient Alphabets Level Series

Travis Wayne Goodsell
1/29/2016

The correct translation begins with a correct understanding of the alphabet.

For it is by my completed works that you shall know me...

Author's Note

I've been working on the ancient alphabets since 1996. After making my discovery of the origins of the alphabets I've done a lot of research which is all published. But with the popularity of the interest in the ancient languages has inspired me to redesign my publications to make it simpler for others to understand and to take the learner through the various levels of understanding. Then I got inspiration to expand the level system to include a simplification of the scientific research process. So because of the numerous books I then got inspired to turn my note papers into a publication for others to use as a checklist for their own personal library. Obviously I haven't published all of the books listed, but it is a listing of all of the books I will publish this year, so you can keep watch for what you are looking for.

ALPHABETS

LEVEL 1
Letters

[ ] Paleo-Hebrew, vol. 1

[ ] Paleo-Greek, vol. 2

[ ] Hebrew, vol. 3

[ ] Greek, vol. 4

[ ] Aramaic, vol. 5

[ ] Ancient Alphabets Combined Level Series, vol. 5

ALPHABETS

LEVEL 2
Names

[ ] Paleo-Hebrew, vol. 1

[ ] Paleo-Greek, vol. 2

[ ] Hebrew, vol. 3

[ ] Greek, vol. 4

[ ] Aramaic, vol. 5

[ ] Ancient Alphabets Combined Level Series, vol. 5

ALPHABETS

LEVEL 3
Phonemes

[ ] Paleo-Hebrew, vol. 1

[ ] Paleo-Greek, vol. 2

[ ] Hebrew, vol. 3

[ ] Greek, vol. 4

[ ] Aramaic, vol. 5

[ ] Ancient Alphabets Combined Level Series, vol. 5

ALPHABETS

LEVEL 4
Egyptian Hieroglyphic Matches

[ ] Paleo-Hebrew, vol. 1

[ ] Paleo-Greek, vol. 2

[ ] Hebrew, vol. 3

[ ] Greek, vol. 4

[ ] Aramaic, vol. 5

[ ] Ancient Alphabets Combined Level Series, vol. 5

ALPHABETS

LEVEL 5
Deity Matches

[ ] Paleo-Hebrew, vol. 1

[ ] Paleo-Greek, vol. 2

[ ] Hebrew, vol. 3

[ ] Greek, vol. 4

[ ] Aramaic, vol. 5

[ ] Ancient Alphabets Combined Level Series, vol. 5

ALPHABETS

LEVEL 6
Etymology

[ ] Paleo-Hebrew, vol. 1

[ ] Paleo-Greek, vol. 2

[ ] Hebrew, vol. 3

[ ] Greek, vol. 4

[ ] Aramaic, vol. 5

[ ] Ancient Alphabets Combined Level Series, vol. 5

ALPHABETS

LEVEL 7
Gematria

[] Paleo-Hebrew, vol. 1

[] Paleo-Greek, vol. 2

[] Hebrew, vol. 3

[] Greek, vol. 4

[] Aramaic, vol. 5

[] Ancient Alphabets Combined Level Series, vol. 5

ALPHABETS
Combination Levels 2 & 3

[ ] Paleo-Hebrew, vol. 1
[ ] Paleo-Greek, vol. 1
[ ] Hebrew, vol. 1
[ ] Greek, vol. 1
[ ] Aramaic, vol. 1
[ ] Proto Sinaitic
[ ] Ancient Alphabet Combinations Combined Level Series, vol. 1

Combination Levels 1-4

[ ] Paleo-Hebrew, vol. 2
[ ] Paleo-Greek, vol. 2
[ ] Hebrew, vol. 2
[ ] Greek, vol. 2
[ ] Aramaic, vol. 2
[ ] Ancient Alphabet Combinations Combined Level Series, vol. 2

Combination Levels 1-5

[ ] Paleo-Hebrew, vol. 3
[ ] Paleo-Greek, vol. 3
[ ] Hebrew, vol. 3
[ ] Greek, vol. 3
[ ] Aramaic, vol. 3
[ ] Ancient Alphabet Combinations Combined Level Series, vol. 3

Combination Levels 1-6

[ ] Paleo-Hebrew, vol. 4
[ ] Paleo-Greek, vol. 4
[ ] Hebrew, vol. 4
[ ] Greek, vol. 4
[ ] Aramaic, vol. 4
[ ] Ancient Alphabet Combinations Combined Level Series, vol. 4

Combination Levels 1-7

[ ] Paleo-Hebrew, vol. 4
[ ] Paleo-Greek, vol. 4
[ ] Hebrew, vol. 4
[ ] Greek, vol. 4
[ ] Aramaic, vol. 4
[ ] Ancient Alphabet Combinations Combined Level Series, vol. 4

ALPHABETS

LEVEL 1

Paleo-Hebrew Letter Comparisons

[ ] Paleo-Hebrew letters compared with Paleo-Greek, vol. 1
[ ] Paleo-Hebrew letters compared with Hebrew, vol. 2
[ ] Paleo-Hebrew letters compared with Greek, vol. 3
[ ] Paleo-Hebrew letters compared with Aramaic, vol. 4
[ ] Paleo-Hebrew letters compared with Proto Si-aitic, vol. 5
[ ] Combined Level 1 1 Paleo-Hebrew Comparisons

LEVEL 1

Paleo-Greek Letter Comparisons

[ ] Paleo-Greek letters compared with Paleo-Hebrew, vol. 1
[ ] Paleo-Greek letters compared with Hebrew, vol. 2
[ ] Paleo-Greek letters compared with Greek, vol 3
[ ] Paleo-Greek letters compared with Aramaic, vol. 4
[ ] Paleo-Greek letters compared with Proto Sinaitic, vol. 5
[ ] Combined Level 1 Paleo-Greek Comparisons

LEVEL 1

Hebrew Letter Comparisons

[ ] Hebrew letters compared with Paleo-Hebrew, vol. 1
[ ] Hebrew letters compared with Paleo-Greek, vol. 2
[ ] Hebrew letters compared with Greek vol. 3
[ ] Hebrew letters compared with Aramaic, vol. 4
[ ] Hebrew letters compared with Proto Sinaitic, vol. 5
[ ] Combined Level 1 Hebrew Comparisons

LEVEL 1

Greek Letter Comparisons

[ ] Greek letters compared with Paleo-Hebrew, vol. 1
[ ] Greek letters compared with Paleo-Greek, vo. 2
[ ] Greek letters compared with Hebrew, vol. 3
[ ] Greek letters compared with Aramaic, vol. 4
[ ] Greek letters compared with Proto Sinaitic, vol. 5
[ ] Combined Level 1 Greek Comparisons

LEVEL 1
Aramaic Letter Comparisons

[ ] Aramaic letters compared with Paleo-Hebrew, vol. 1

[ ] Aramaic letters compared with Paleo-Greek, vol. 2

[ ] Aramaic letters compared with Hebrew, vol. 3

[ ] Aramaic letters compared with Greek, vol. 4

[ ] Aramaic letters compared with Proto Sinaitic, vol. 5

[ ] Combined Level 1 1 Aramaic Comparisons

LEVEL 1
Proto Sinaitic Letter Comparisons

[ ] Proto Sinaitic letters compared with Paleo-Hebrew, vol. 1

[ ] Proto Sinaitic letters compared with Paleo-Greek, vol. 2

[ ] Proto Sinaitic letters compared with Hebrew, vol. 3

[ ] Proto Sinaitic letters compared with Greek, vol. 4

[ ] Proto Sinaitic letters compared with Aramaic, vol. 5

[ ] Combined level 1 Proto Sinaitic Comparisons

ALPHABETS
LEVEL 2
Paleo-Hebrew Name Comparisons

[ ] Paleo-Hebrew names compared with Paleo-Greek, vol. 1

[ ] Paleo-Hebrew names compared with Hebrew, vol. 2

[ ] Paleo-Hebrew names compared with Greek, vol. 3

[ ] Paleo-Hebrew names compared with Aramaic, vol. 4

[ ] Paleo-Hebrew names compared with Proto Sinaitic, vol. 5

[ ] Combined Level 2 Paleo-Hebrew Comparisons

LEVEL 2
Paleo-Greek Name Comparisons

[ ] Paleo-Greek names compared with Paleo-Hebrew, vol. 1

[ ] Paleo-Greek names compared with Hebrew, vol. 2

[ ] Paleo-Greek names compared with Greek, vol. 3

[ ] Paleo-Greek names compared with Aramaic, vol. 4

[ ] Paleo-Greek names compared with Proto Sinaitic, vol. 5

[ ] Combined Level 2 Paleo-Greek Comparisons

LEVEL 2
Hebrew Name Comparisons

[ ] Hebrew names compared with Paleo-Hebrew, vol. 1

[ ] Hebrew names compared with Paleo-Greek, vol. 2

[ ] Hebrew names compared with Greek vol. 3

[ ] Hebrew names compared with Aramaic, vol. 4

[ ] Hebrew names compared with Proto Sinaitic, vol. 5

[ ] Combined Level 2 Hebrew Comparisons

LEVEL 2
Greek Name Comparisons

[ ] Greek names compared with Paleo-Hebrew, vol. 1

[ ] Greek names compared with Paleo-Greek, vol. 2

[ ] Greek names compared with Hebrew, vol. 3

[ ] Greek names compared with Aramaic, vol. 4

[ ] Greek names compared with Proto Sinaitic, vol. 5

[ ] Combined Level 2 Greek Comparisons

LEVEL 2
Aramaic Name Comparisons

[ ] Aramaic names compared with Paleo-Hebrew, vol. 1

[ ] Aramaic names compared with Paleo-Greek, vol. 2

[ ] Aramaic names compared with Hebrew, vol. 3

[ ] Aramaic names compared with Greek, vol. 4

[ ] Aramaic names compared with Proto Sinaitic, vol. 5

[ ] Combined Level 2 Aramaic Comparisons

LEVEL 2
Proto Sinaitic Name Comparisons

[ ] Proto Sinaitic names compared with Paleo-Hebrew, vol. 1

[ ] Proto Sinaitic names compared with Paleo-Greek, vol. 2

[ ] Proto Sinaitic names compared with Hebrew, vol. 3

[ ] Proto Sinaitic names compared with Greek, vol. 4

[ ] Proto Sinaitic names compared with Aramaic, vol. 5

[ ] Combined level 2 Proto Sinaitic Comparisons

ALPHABETS
LEVEL 3
Paleo-Hebrew Phoneme Comparisons

[ ] Paleo-Hebrew phonemes compared with Paleo-Greek, vol. 1

[ ] Paleo-Hebrew phonemes compared with Hebrew, vol. 2

[ ] Paleo-Hebrew phonemes compared with Greek, vol. 3

[ ] Paleo-Hebrew phonemes compared with Aramaic, vol. 4

[ ] Paleo-Hebrew phonemes compared with Proto Sinaitic, vol. 5

[ ] Combined Level 3 Paleo-Hebrew Comparisons

LEVEL 3
Paleo-Greek Phoneme Comparisons

[ ] Paleo-Greek phonemes compared with Paleo-Hebrew, vol. 1

[ ] Paleo-Greek phonemes compared with Hebrew, vol. 2

[ ] Paleo-Greek phonemes compared with Greek, vol. 3

[ ] Paleo-Greek phonemes compared with Aramaic, vol. 4

[ ] Paleo-Greek phonemes compared with Proto Sinaitic, vol. 5

[ ] Combined Level 3 Paleo-Greek Comparisons

LEVEL 3
Hebrew Phoneme Comparisons

[ ] Hebrew phonemes compared with Paleo-Hebrew, vol. 1

[ ] Hebrew phonemes compared with Paleo-Greek, vol. 2

[ ] Hebrew phonemes compared with Greek, vol. 3

[ ] Hebrew phonemes compared with Aramaic, vol. 4

[ ] Hebrew phonemes compared with Proto Sinaitic, vol. 5

[ ] Combined Level 3 Hebrew Comparisons

LEVEL 3
Greek Phoneme Comparisons

[ ] Greek phonemes compared with Paleo-Hebrew, vol. 1

[ ] Greek phonemes compared with Paleo-Greek, vol. 2

[ ] Greek phonemes compared with Hebrew, vol. 3

[ ] Greek phonemes compared with Aramaic, vol. 4

[ ] Greek phonemes compared with Proto Sinaitic, vol. 5

[ ] Combined Level 3 Greek Comparisons

LEVEL 3
Aramaic Phoneme Comparisons

[ ] Aramaic phonemes compared with Paleo-Hebrew, vol. 1

[ ] Aramaic phonemes compared with Paleo-Greek, vol. 2

[ ] Aramaic phonemes compared with Hebrew, vol. 3

[ ] Aramaic phonemes compared with Greek, vol. 4

[ ] Aramaic phonemes compared with Proto Sinaitic, vol. 5

[ ] Combined Level 3 Aramaic Comparisons

LEVEL 3
Proto Sinaitic Phoneme Comparisons

[ ] Proto Sinaitic phonemes compared with Paleo-Hebrew, vol. 1

[ ] Proto Sinaitic phonemes compared with Paleo-Greek, vol. 2

[ ] Proto Sinaitic phonemes compared with Hebrew, vol. 3

[ ] Proto Sinaitic phonemes compared with Greek, vol. 4

[ ] Proto Sinaitic phonemes compared with Aramaic, vol. 5

[ ] Combined level 3 Proto Sinaitic Comparisons

ALPHABETS
LEVEL 4
Paleo-Hebrew Egyptian Hieroglyphic Match Comparisons

[ ] Paleo-Hebrew Egyptian Hieroglyphic matches compared with Paleo-Greek, vol. 1
[ ] Paleo-Hebrew Egyptian Hieroglyphic matches compared with Hebrew, vol. 2
[ ] Paleo-Hebrew Egyptian Hieroglyphic matches compared with Greek, vol. 3
[ ] Paleo-Hebrew Egyptian Hieroglyphic matches compared with Aramaic, vol. 4
[ ] Combined Level 4 Paleo-Hebrew Comparisons

LEVEL 4
Paleo-Greek Egyptian Hieroglyphic Match Comparisons

[ ] Paleo-Greek Egyptian Hieroglyphic matches compared with Paleo-Hebrew, vol. 1
[ ] Paleo-Greek Egyptian Hieroglyphic matches compared with Hebrew, vol. 2
[ ] Paleo-Greek Egyptian Hieroglyphic matches compared with Greek, vol. 3
[ ] Paleo-Greek Egyptian Hieroglyphic matches compared with Aramaic, vol. 4
[ ] Combined Level 4 Paleo-Greek Comparisons

LEVEL 4
Hebrew Egyptian Hieroglyphic Match Comparisons

[ ] Hebrew Egyptian Hieroglyphic matches compared with Paleo-Hebrew, vol. 1
[ ] Hebrew Egyptian Hieroglyphic matches compared with Paleo-Greek, vol. 2
[ ] Hebrew Egyptian Hieroglyphic matches compared with Greek, vol. 3
[ ] Hebrew Egyptian Hieroglyphic matches compared with Aramaic, vol. 4
[ ] Combined Level 4 Hebrew Comparisons

LEVEL 4
Greek Egyptian Hieroglyphic Match Comparisons

[ ] Greek Egyptian Hieroglyphic matches compared with Paleo-Hebrew, vol. 1
[ ] Greek Egyptian Hieroglyphic matches compared with Paleo-Greek, vol. 2
[ ] Greek Egyptian Hieroglyphic matches compared with Hebrew, vol. 3
[ ] Greek Egyptian Hieroglyphic matches compared with Aramaic, vol. 4
[ ] Combined Level 4 Greek Comparisons

LEVEL 4
Aramaic Egyptian Hieroglyphic Match Comparisons

[ ] Aramaic Egyptian Hieroglyphic matches compared with Paleo-Hebrew, vol. 1
[ ] Aramaic Egyptian Hieroglyphic matches compared with Paleo-Greek, vol. 2
[ ] Aramaic Egyptian Hieroglyphic matches compared with Hebrew, vol. 3
[ ] Aramaic Egyptian Hieroglyphic matches compared with Greek, vol. 4
[ ] Combined Level 4 Aramaic Comparisons

ALPHABETS
LEVEL 5
Paleo-Hebrew Deity Match Comparisons

[ ] Paleo-Hebrew Deity matches compared with Paleo-Greek, vol. 1

[ ] Paleo-Hebrew Deity matches compared with Hebrew, vol. 2

[ ] Paleo-Hebrew Deity matches compared with Greek, vol. 3

[ ] Paleo-Hebrew Deity matches compared with Aramaic, vol. 4

[ ] Combined Level 5 Paleo-Hebrew Comparisons

LEVEL 5
Paleo-Greek Deity Match Comparisons

[ ] Paleo-Greek Deity matches compared with Paleo-Hebrew, vol. 1

[ ] Paleo-Greek Deity matches compared with Hebrew, vol. 2

[ ] Paleo-Greek Deity matches compared with Greek, vol. 3

[ ] Paleo-Greek Deity matches compared with Aramaic, vol. 4

[ ] Combined Level 5 Paleo-Greek Comparisons

LEVEL 5
Hebrew Deity Match Comparisons

[ ] Hebrew Deity matches compared with Paleo-Hebrew, vol. 1

[ ] Hebrew Deity matches compared with Paleo-Greek, vol. 2

[ ] Hebrew Deity matches compared with Greek, vol. 3

[ ] Hebrew Deity matches compared with Aramaic, vol. 4

[ ] Combined Level 5 Hebrew Comparisons

LEVEL 5
Greek Deity Match Comparisons

[ ] Greek Deity matches compared with Paleo-Hebrew, vol. 1

[ ] Greek Deity matches compared with Paleo-Greek, vol. 2

[ ] Greek Deity matches compared with Hebrew, vol. 3

[ ] Greek Deity matches compared with Aramaic, vol. 4

[ ] Combined Level 5 Greek Comparisons

LEVEL 5
Aramaic Deity Match Comparisons

[ ] Aramaic Deity matches compared with Paleo-Hebrew, vol. 1

[ ] Aramaic Deity matches compared with Paleo-Greek, vol. 2

[ ] Aramaic Deity matches compared with Hebrew, vol. 3

[ ] Aramaic Deity matches compared with Greek, vol. 4

[ ] Combined Level 5 Aramaic Comparisons

ALPHABETS

LEVEL 6
Paleo-Hebrew Etymology Comparisons

[] Paleo-Hebrew etymology compared with Paleo-Greek, vol. 1

[] Paleo-Hebrew etymology compared with Hebrew, vol. 2

[] Paleo-Hebrew etymology compared with Greek, vol. 3

[] Paleo-Hebrew etymology compared with Aramaic, vol. 4

[] Combined Level 6 Paleo-Hebrew Comparisons

LEVEL 6
Paleo-Greek Etymology Comparisons

[] Paleo-Greek etymology compared with Paleo-Hebrew, vol. 1

[] Paleo-Greek etymology compared with Hebrew, vol. 2

[] Paleo-Greek etymology compared with Greek, vol. 3

[] Paleo-Greek etymology compared with Aramaic, vol. 4

[] Combined Level 6 Paleo-Greek Comparisons

LEVEL 6
Hebrew Etymology Comparisons

[] Hebrew etymology compared with Paleo-Hebrew, vol. 1

[] Hebrew etymology compared with Paleo-Greek, vol. 2

[] Hebrew etymology compared with Greek, vol. 3

[] Hebrew etymology compared with Aramaic, vol. 4

[] Combined Level 6 Hebrew Comparisons

LEVEL 6
Greek Etymology Comparisons

[] Greek etymology compared with Paleo-Hebrew, vol. 1

[] Greek etymology compared with Paleo-Greek vol. 2

[] Greek etymology compared with Hebrew, vol. 3

[] Greek etymology compared with Aramaic, vol. 4

[] Combined Level 6 Greek Comparisons

LEVEL 6
Aramaic Etymology Comparisons

[] Aramaic etymology compared with Paleo-Hebrew, vol. 1

[] Aramaic etymology compared with Paleo-Greek, vol. 2

[] Aramaic etymology compared with Hebrew, vol. 3

[] Aramaic etymology compared with Greek, vol. 4

[] Combined Level 6 Aramaic Comparisons

ALPHABETS
LEVEL 7
Paleo-Hebrew Gematria Comparisons

[ ] Paleo-Hebrew Gematria compared with Paleo-Greek, vol. 1

[ ] Paleo-Hebrew Gematria compared with Hebrew, vol. 2

[ ] Paleo-Hebrew Gematria compared with Greek, vol. 3

[ ] Paleo-Hebrew Gematria compared with Aramaic, vol. 4

[ ] Paleo-Hebrew Gematria compared with Proto Sinaitic, vol. 5

[ ] Combined Level 7 Paleo-Hebrew Comparisons

LEVEL 7
Paleo-Greek Gematria Comparisons

[ ] Paleo-Greek Gematria compared with Paleo-Hebrew, vol. 1

[ ] Paleo-Greek Gematria compared with Hebrew, vol. 2

[ ] Paleo-Greek Gematria compared with Greek, vol. 3

[ ] Paleo-Greek Gematria compared with Aramaic, vol. 4

[ ] Paleo-Greek Gematria compared with Proto Sinaitic, vol. 5

[ ] Combined Level 7 Paleo-Greek Comparisons

LEVEL 7
Hebrew Gematria Comparisons

[ ] Hebrew Gematria compared with Paleo-Hebrew, vol. 1

[ ] Hebrew Gematria compared with Paleo-Greek, vol. 2

[ ] Hebrew Gematria compared with Greek, vol. 3

[ ] Hebrew Gematria compared with Aramaic, vol. 4

[ ] Hebrew Gematria compared with Proto Sinaitic, vol. 5

[ ] Combined Level 7 Hebrew Comparisons

LEVEL 7
Greek Gematria Comparisons

[ ] Greek Gematria compared with Paleo-Hebrew, vol. 1

[ ] Greek Gematria compared with Paleo-Greek, vol. 2

[ ] Greek Gematria compared with Hebrew, vol. 3

[ ] Greek Gematria compared with Aramaic, vol. 4

[ ] Greek Gematria compared with Proto Sinaitic, vol. 5

[ ] Combined Level 7 Greek Comparisons

LEVEL 7
Aramaic Gematria Comparisons

[ ] Aramaic Gematria compared with Paleo-Hebrew, vol. 1

[ ] Aramaic Gematria compared with Paleo-Greek, vol. 2

[ ] Aramaic Gematria compared with Hebrew, vol. 3

[ ] Aramaic Gematria compared with Greek, vol. 4

[ ] Aramaic Gematria compared with Proto Sinaitic, vol. 5

[ ] Combined Level 7 Aramaic Comparsons

LEVEL 7
Proto Sinaitic Gematria Comparisons

[ ] Proto Sinaitic Gematria compared with Paleo-Hebrew, vol. 1

[ ] Proto Sinaitic Gematria compared with Paleo-Greek, vol. 2

[ ] Proto Sinaitic Gematria compared with Hebrew, vol. 3

[ ] Proto Sinaitic Gematria compared with Greek, vol. 4

[ ] Proto Sinaitic Gematria compared with Aramaic, vol. 5

[ ] Combined level 7 Proto Sinaitic Comparisons

ALPHABETS
LEVEL 1
Paleo-Hebrew Letter Comparisons

[ ] Paleo-Greek letters compared with Paleo-Hebrew, vol. 1

[ ] Hebrew letters compared with Paleo-Hebrew, vol. 2

[ ] Greek letters compared with Paleo-Hebrew, vol. 3

[ ] Aramaic letters compared with Paleo-Hebrew, vol. 4

[ ] Proto Sinaitic letters compared with Paleo-Hebrew, vol. 5

[ ] Combined Level 1 Paleo-Hebrew Comparisons

LEVEL 1
Paleo-Greek Letter Comparisons

[ ] Paleo-Hebrew letters compared with Paleo-Greek, vol. 1

[ ] Hebrew letters compared with Paleo-Greek, vol. 2

[ ] Greek letters compared with Paleo-Greek, vol. 3

[ ] Aramaic letters compared with Paleo-Greek, vol. 4

[ ] Proto Sinaitic letters compared with Paleo-Greek, vol. 5

[ ] Combined Level 1 Paleo-Greek Comparisons

LEVEL 1
Hebrew Letter Comparisons

[ ] Paleo-Hebrew letters compared with Hebrew, vol. 1

[ ] Paleo-Greek letters compared with Hebrew, vol. 2

[ ] Greek letters compared with Hebrew, vol. 3

[ ] Aramaic letters compared with Hebrew, vol. 4

[ ] Proto Sinaitic letters compared with Hebrew, vol. 5

[ ] Combined Level 1 Hebrew Comparisons

LEVEL 1
Greek Letter Comparisons

[ ] Paleo-Hebrew letters compared with Greek, vol. 1

[ ] Paleo-Greek letters compared with Greek, vol. 2

[ ] Hebrew letters compared with Greek, vol. 3

[ ] Aramaic letters compared with Greek, vol. 4

[ ] Proto Sinaitic letters compared with Greek, vol. 5

[ ] Combined Level 1 Greek Comparisons

LEVEL 1
Aramaic Letter Comparisons

[] Paleo-Hebrew letters compared with Aramaic, vol. 1

[] Paleo-Greek letters compared with Aramaic, vol. 2

[] Hebrew letters compared with Aramaic, vol. 3

[] Greek letters compared with Aramaic, vol. 4

[] Proto Sinaitic letters compared with Aramaic, vol. 5

[] Combined Level 1 Aramaic Comparisons

LEVEL 1
Proto Sinaitic Letter Comparisons

[] Paleo-Hebrew letters compared with Proto Sinaitic, vol. 1

[] Paleo-Greek letters compared with Proto Sinaitic, vol. 2

[] Hebrew letters compared with Proto Sinaitic, vol. 3

[] Greek letters compared with Proto Sinaitic, vol. 4

[] Aramaic letters compared with Proto Sinaitic, vol. 5

[] Combined level 1 Proto Sinaitic Comparisons

ALPHABETS

LEVEL 2

Paleo-Hebrew Name Comparisons

[ ] Paleo-Greek names compared with Paleo-Hebrew, vol. 1

[ ] Hebrew names compared with Paleo-Hebrew, vol. 2

[ ] Greek names compared with Paleo-Hebrew, vol. 3

[ ] Aramaic names compared with Paleo-Hebrew, vol. 4

[ ] Proto Sinaitic names compared with Paleo-Hebrew, vol. 5

[ ] Combined Level 2 Paleo-Hebrew Comparisons

LEVEL 2

Paleo-Greek Name Comparisons

[ ] Paleo-Hebrew names compared with Paleo-Greek, vol. 1

[ ] Hebrew names compared with Paleo-Greek, vol. 2

[ ] Greek names compared with Paleo-Greek, vol. 3

[ ] Aramaic names compared with Paleo-Greek, vol. 4

[ ] Proto Sinaitic names compared with Paleo-Greek, vol. 5

[ ] Combined Level 2 Paleo-Greek Comparisons

LEVEL 2

Hebrew Name Comparisons

[ ] Paleo-Hebrew names compared with Hebrew, vol. 1

[ ] Paleo-Greek names compared with Hebrew, vol. 2

[ ] Greek names compared with Hebrew, vol. 3

[ ] Aramaic names compared with Hebrew, vol. 4

[ ] Proto Sinaitic names compared with Hebrew, vol. 5

[ ] Combined Level 2 Hebrew Comparisons

LEVEL 2

Greek Name Comparisons

[ ] Paleo-Hebrew names compared with Greek, vol. 1

[ ] Paleo-Greek names compared with Greek, vol. 2

[ ] Hebrew names compared with Greek, vol. 3

[ ] Aramaic names compared with Greek, vol. 4

[ ] Proto Sinaitic names compared with Greek, vol. 5

[ ] Combined Level 2 Greek Comparisons

LEVEL 2
Aramaic Name Comparisons

[ ] Paleo-Hebrew names compared with Aramaic, vol. 1

[ ] Paleo-Greek names compared with Aramaic, vol. 2

[ ] Hebrew names compared with Aramaic, vol. 3

[ ] Greek names compared with Aramaic, vol. 4

[ ] Proto Sinaitic names compared with Aramaic, vol. 5

[ ] Combined Level 2 Aramaic Comparisons

LEVEL 2
Proto Sinaitic Name Comparisons

[ ] Paleo-Hebrew names compared with Proto Sinaitic, vol. 1

[ ] Paleo-Greek names compared with Proto Siraitic, vol. 2

[ ] Hebrew names compared with Proto Sinaitic, vol. 3

[ ] Greek names compared with Proto Sinaitic, vol. 4

[ ] Aramaic names compared with Proto Sinaitic, vol. 5

[ ] Combined level 2 Proto Sinaitic Comparisons

ALPHABETS
LEVEL 3
Paleo-Hebrew Phoneme Comparisons

[ ] Paleo-Greek phonemes compared with Paleo-Hebrew, vol. 1

[ ] Hebrew phonemes compared with Paleo-Hebrew, vol. 2

[ ] Greek phonemes compared with Paleo-Hebrew, vol. 3

[ ] Aramaic phonemes compared with Paleo-Hebrew, vol. 4

[ ] Proto Sinaitic phonemes compared with Paleo-Hebrew, vol. 5

[ ] Combined Level 3 Paleo-Hebrew Comparisons

LEVEL 3
Paleo-Greek Phoneme Comparisons

[ ] Paleo-Hebrew phonemes compared with Paleo-Greek, vol. 1

[ ] Hebrew phonemes compared with Paleo-Greek, vol. 2

[ ] Greek phonemes compared with Paleo-Greek, vol. 3

[ ] Aramaic phonemes compared with Paleo-Greek, vol. 4

[ ] Proto Sinaitic phonemes compared with Paleo-Greek, vol. 5

[ ] Combined Level 3 Paleo-Greek Comparisons

LEVEL 3
Hebrew Phoneme Comparisons

[ ] Paleo-Hebrew phonemes compared with Hebrew, vol. 1

[ ] Paleo-Greek phonemes compared with Hebrew, vol. 2

[ ] Greek phonemes compared with Hebrew, vol. 3

[ ] Aramaic phonemes compared with Hebrew, vol. 4

[ ] Proto Sinaitic phonemes compared with Hebrew, vol. 5

[ ] Combined Level 3 Hebrew Comparisons

LEVEL 3
Greek Phoneme Comparisons

[ ] Paleo-Hebrew phonemes compared with Greek, vol. 1

[ ] Paleo-Greek phonemes compared with Greek, vol. 2

[ ] Hebrew phonemes compared with Greek, vol. 3

[ ] Aramaic phonemes compared with Greek, vol. 4

[ ] Proto Sinaitic phonemes compared with Greek, vol. 5

[ ] Combined Level 3 Greek Comparisons

LEVEL 3
Aramaic Phoneme Comparisons

[ ] Paleo-Hebrew phonemes compared with Aramaic, vol. 1

[ ] Paleo-Greek phonemes compared with Aramaic, vol. 2

[ ] Hebrew phonemes compared with Aramaic, vol. 3

[ ] Greek phonemes compared with Aramaic, vol. 4

[ ] Proto Sinaitic phonemes compared with Aramaic, vol. 5

[ ] Combined Level 3 Aramaic Comparisons

LEVEL 3
Proto Sinaitic Phoneme Comparisons

[ ] Paleo-Hebrew phonemes compared with Proto Sinaitic, vol. 1

[ ] Paleo-Greek phonemes compared with Proto Sinaitic, vol. 2

[ ] Hebrew phonemes compared with Proto Sinaitic, vol. 3

[ ] Greek phonemes compared with Proto Sinaitic, vol. 4

[ ] Aramaic phonemes compared with Proto Sinaitic, vol. 5

[ ] Combined level 3 Proto Sinaitic Comparisons

ALPHABETS
LEVEL 4
Paleo-Hebrew Egyptian Hieroglyphic Match Comparisons

[ ] Paleo-Greek Egyptian Hieroglyphic Matches compared with Paleo-Hebrew, vol. 1

[ ] Hebrew Egyptian Hieroglyphic Matches compared with Paleo-Hebrew, vol. 2

[ ] Greek Egyptian Hieroglyphic Matches compared with Paleo-Hebrew, vol. 3

[ ] Aramaic Egyptian Hieroglyphic Matches compared with Paleo-Hebrew, vol. 4

[ ] Combined Level 4 Paleo-Hebrew Comparisons

LEVEL 4
Paleo-Greek Egyptian Hieroglyphic Match Comparisons

[ ] Paleo-Hebrew Egyptian Hieroglyphic Matches compared with Paleo-Greek, vol. 1

[ ] Hebrew Egyptian Hieroglyphic Matches compared with Paleo-Greek, vol. 2

[ ] Greek Egyptian Hieroglyphic Matches compared with Paleo-Greek, vol. 3

[ ] Aramaic Egyptian Hieroglyphic Matches compared with Paleo-Greek, vol. 4

[ ] Combined Level 4 Paleo-Greek Comparisons

LEVEL 4
Hebrew Egyptian Hieroglyphic Match Comparisons

[ ] Paleo-Hebrew Egyptian Hieroglyphic Matches compared with Hebrew, vol. 1

[ ] Paleo-Greek Egyptian Hieroglyphic Matches compared with Hebrew, vol. 2

[ ] Greek Egyptian Hieroglyphic Matches compared with Hebrew, vol. 3

[ ] Aramaic Egyptian Hieroglyphic Matches compared with Hebrew, vol. 4

[ ] Combined Level 4 Hebrew Comparisons

LEVEL 4
Greek Egyptian Hieroglyphic Match Comparisons

[ ] Paleo-Hebrew Egyptian Hieroglyphic Matches compared with Greek, vol. 1

[ ] Paleo-Greek Egyptian Hieroglyphic Matches compared with Greek, vol. 2

[ ] Hebrew Egyptian Hieroglyphic Matches compared with Greek, vol. 3

[ ] Aramaic Egyptian Hieroglyphic Matches compared with Greek, vol. 4

[ ] Combined Level 4 Greek Comparisons

LEVEL 4
Aramaic Egyptian Hieroglyphic Match Comparisons

[ ] Paleo-Hebrew Egyptian Hieroglyphic Matches compared with Aramaic, vol. 1

[ ] Paleo-Greek Egyptian Hieroglyphic Matches compared with Aramaic, vol. 2

[ ] Hebrew Egyptian Hieroglyphic Matches compared with Aramaic, vol. 3

[ ] Greek Egyptian Hieroglyphic Matches compared with Aramaic, vol. 4

[ ] Combined Level 4 Aramaic Comparisons

ALPHABETS
LEVEL 5
Paleo-Hebrew Deity Match Comparisons

[ ] Paleo-Greek Deity matches compared with Paleo-Hebrew, vol. 1

[ ] Hebrew Deity matches compared with Paleo-Hebrew, vol. 2

[ ] Greek Deity matches compared with Paleo-Hebrew, vol. 3

[ ] Aramaic Deity matches compared with Paleo-Hebrew, vol. 4

[ ] Combined Level 5 Paleo-Hebrew Comparisons

LEVEL 5
Paleo-Greek Deity Match Comparisons

[ ] Paleo-Hebrew Deity matches compared with Paleo-Greek, vol. 1

[ ] Hebrew Deity matches compared with Paleo-Greek, vol. 2

[ ] Greek Deity matches compared with Paleo-Greek, vol. 3

[ ] Aramaic Deity matches compared with Paleo-Greek, vol. 4

[ ] Combined Level 5 Paleo-Greek Comparisons

LEVEL 5
Hebrew Deity Match Comparisons

[ ] Paleo-Hebrew Deity matches compared with Hebrew, vol. 1

[ ] Paleo-Greek Deity matches compared with Hebrew, vol. 2

[ ] Greek Deity matches compared with Hebrew, vol. 3

[ ] Aramaic Deity matches compared with Hebrew, vol. 4

[ ] Combined Level 5 Hebrew Comparisons

LEVEL 5
Greek Deity Match Comparisons

[ ] Paleo-Hebrew Deity matches compared with Greek, vol. 1

[ ] Paleo-Greek Deity matches compared with Greek, vol. 2

[ ] Hebrew Deity matches compared with Greek, vol. 3

[ ] Aramaic Deity matches compared with Greek, vol. 4

[ ] Combined Level 5 Greek Comparisons

LEVEL 5
Aramaic Deity Match Comparisons

[ ] Paleo-Hebrew Deity matches compared with Aramaic, vol. 1

[ ] Paleo-Greek Deity matches compared with Aramaic, vol. 2

[ ] Hebrew Deity matches compared with Aramaic, vol. 3

[ ] Greek Deity matches compared with Aramaic, vol. 4

[ ] Combined Level 5 Aramaic Comparisons

ALPHABETS

LEVEL 6
Paleo-Hebrew Etymology Comparisons

[ ] Paleo-Greek etymology compared with Paleo-Hebrew, vol. 1

[ ] Hebrew etymology compared with Paleo-Hebrew, vol. 2

[ ] Greek etymology compared with Paleo-Hebrew, vol. 3

[ ] Aramaic etymology compared with Paleo-Hebrew, vol. 4

[ ] Combined Level 6 Paleo-Hebrew Comparisons

LEVEL 6
Paleo-Greek Etymology Comparisons

[ ] Paleo-Hebrew etymology compared with Paleo-Greek, vol. 1

[ ] Hebrew etymology compared with Paleo-Greek, vol. 2

[ ] Greek etymology compared with Paleo-Greek, vol. 3

[ ] Aramaic etymology compared with Paleo-Greek, vol. 4

[ ] Combined Level 6 Paleo-Greek Comparisons

LEVEL 6
Hebrew Etymology Comparisons

[ ] Paleo-Hebrew etymology compared with Hebrew, vol. 1

[ ] Paleo-Greek etymology compared with Hebrew, vol. 2

[ ] Greek etymology compared with Hebrew, vol. 3

[ ] Aramaic etymology compared with Hebrew, vol. 4

[ ] Combined Level 6 Hebrew Comparisons

LEVEL 6
Greek Etymology Comparisons

[ ] Paleo-Hebrew etymology compared with Greek, vol. 1

[ ] Paleo-Greek etymology compared with Greek, vol. 2

[ ] Hebrew etymology compared with Greek, vol. 3

[ ] Aramaic etymology compared with Greek, vol. 4

[ ] Combined Level 6 Greek Comparisons

LEVEL 6
Aramaic Etymology Comparisons

[ ] Paleo-Hebrew etymology compared with Aramaic, vol. 1

[ ] Paleo-Greek etymology compared with Aramaic, vol. 2

[ ] Hebrew etymology compared with Aramaic, vol. 3

[ ] Greek etymology compared with Aramaic, vol. 4

[ ] Combined Level 6 Aramaic Comparisons

ALPHABETS
LEVEL 7
Paleo-Hebrew Gematria Comparisons

[ ] Paleo-Greek Gematria compared with Paleo-Hebrew, vol. 1

[ ] Hebrew Gematria compared with Paleo-Hebrew, vol. 2

[ ] Greek Gematria compared with Paleo-Hebrew, vol. 3

[ ] Aramaic Gematria compared with Paleo-Hebrew, vol. 4

[ ] Proto Sinaitic Gematria compared with Paleo-Hebrew, vol. 5

[ ] Combined Level 7 Paleo-Hebrew Comparisons

LEVEL 7
Paleo-Greek Gematria Comparisons

[ ] Paleo-Hebrew Gematria compared with Paleo-Greek, vol. 1

[ ] Hebrew Gematria compared with Paleo-Greek, vol. 2

[ ] Greek Gematria compared with Paleo-Greek, vol. 3

[ ] Aramaic Gematria compared with Paleo-Greek, vol. 4

[ ] Proto Sinaitic Gematria compared with Paleo-Greek, vol. 5

[ ] Combined Level 7 Paleo-Greek Comparisons

LEVEL 7
Hebrew Gematria Comparisons

[ ] Paleo-Hebrew Gematria compared with Hebrew, vol. 1

[ ] Paleo-Greek Gematria compared with Hebrew, vol. 2

[ ] Greek Gematria compared with Hebrew, vol. 3

[ ] Aramaic Gematria compared with Hebrew, vol. 4

[ ] Proto Sinaitic Gematria compared with Hebrew, vol. 5

[ ] Combined Level 7 Hebrew Comparisons

LEVEL 7
Greek Gematria Comparisons

[ ] Paleo-Hebrew Gematria compared with Greek, vol. 1

[ ] Paleo-Greek Gematria compared with Greek, vol. 2

[ ] Hebrew Gematria compared with Greek, vol. 3

[ ] Aramaic Gematria compared with Greek, vol. 4

[ ] Proto Sinaitic Gematria compared with Greek, vol. 5

[ ] Combined Level 7 Greek Comparisons

LEVEL 7
Aramaic Gematria Comparisons

[] Paleo-Hebrew Gematria compared with Aramaic, vol. 1

[] Paleo-Greek Gematria compared with Aramaic, vol. 2

[] Hebrew Gematria compared with Aramaic, vol. 3

[] Greek Gematria compared with Aramaic, vol. 4

[] Proto Sinaitic Gematria compared with Aramaic, vol. 5

[] Combined Level 7 Aramaic Comparisons

LEVEL 7
Proto Sinaitic Gematria Comparisons

[] Paleo-Hebrew Gematria compared with Proto Sinaitic, vol. 1

[] Paleo-Greek Gematria compared with Proto Sinaitic, vol. 2

[] Hebrew Gematria compared with Proto Sinaitic, vol. 3

[] Greek Gematria compared with Proto Sinaitic, vol. 4

[] Aramaic Gematria compared with Proto Sinaitic, vol. 5

[] Combined level 7 Proto Sinaitic Comparisons

ALPHABETS

LEVELS 2-3
Paleo-Hebrew Comparisons

[ ] Paleo-Hebrew compared with Paleo-Greek, vol. 1

[ ] Paleo-Hebrew compared with Hebrew, vol. 2

[ ] Paleo-Hebrew compared with Greek, vol. 3

[ ] Paleo-Hebrew compared with Aramaic, vol. 4

[ ] Paleo-Hebrew compared with Proto Sinaitic, vol. 5

[ ] Combined Levels 2-3 Paleo-Hebrew Comparisons

LEVELS 2-3
Paleo-Greek Comparisons

[ ] Paleo-Greek compared with Paleo-Hebrew, vol. 1

[ ] Paleo-Greek compared with Hebrew, vol. 2

[ ] Paleo-Greek compared with Greek, vol. 3

[ ] Paleo-Greek compared with Aramaic, vol. 4

[ ] Paleo-Greek compared with Proto Sinaitic, vol. 5

[ ] Combined Levels 2-3 Paleo-Greek Comparisons

LEVELS 2-3
Hebrew Comparisons

[ ] Hebrew compared with Paleo-Hebrew, vol. 1

[ ] Hebrew compared with Paleo-Greek, vol. 2

[ ] Hebrew compared with Greek, vol. 3

[ ] Hebrew compared with Aramaic, vol. 4

[ ] Hebrew compared with Proto Sinaitic, vol. 5

[ ] Combined Levels 2-3 Hebrew Comparisons

LEVELS 2-3
Greek Comparisons

[ ] Greek compared with Paleo-Hebrew, vol. 1

[ ] Greek compared with Paleo-Greek, vol. 2

[ ] Greek compared with Hebrew, vol. 3

[ ] Greek compared with Aramaic, vol. 4

[ ] Greek compared with Proto Sinaitic, vol. 5

[ ] Combined Levels 2-3 Greek Comparisons

LEVELS 2-3
Aramaic Comparisons

[ ] Aramaic compared with Paleo-Hebrew, vol. 1

[ ] Aramaic compared with Paleo-Greek, vol. 2

[ ] Aramaic compared with Hebrew, vol. 3

[ ] Aramaic compared with Greek, vol. 4

[ ] Aramaic compared with Proto Sinaitic, vol. 5

[ ] Combined Levels 2-3 Aramaic Comparisons

LEVELS 2-3
Proto Sinaitic Comparisons

[ ] Proto Sinaitic compared with Paleo-Hebrew, vol. 1

[ ] Proto Sinaitic compared with Paleo-Greek, vol. 2

[ ] Proto Sinaitic compared with Hebrew, vol. 3

[ ] Proto Sinaitic compared with Greek, vol. 4

[ ] Proto Sinaitic compared with Aramaic, vol. 5

[ ] Combined Levels 2-3 Proto Sinaitic Comparisons

ALPHABETS

LEVELS 1-4
Paleo-Hebrew Comparisons

[ ] Paleo-Hebrew compared with Paleo-Greek, vol. 1

[ ] Paleo-Hebrew compared with Hebrew, vol. 2

[ ] Paleo-Hebrew compared with Greek, vol. 3

[ ] Paleo-Hebrew compared with Aramaic, vol. 4

[ ] Combined Level 1-4 Paleo-Hebrew Comparisons

LEVELS 1-4
Paleo-Greek Comparisons

[ ] Paleo-Greek compared with Paleo-Hebrew, vol. 1

[ ] Paleo-Greek compared with Hebrew, vol. 2

[ ] Paleo-Greek compared with Greek, vol. 3

[ ] Paleo-Greek compared with Aramaic, vol. 4

[ ] Combined Level 1-4 Paleo-Greek Comparisons

LEVELS 1-4
Hebrew Comparisons

[ ] Hebrew compared with Paleo-Hebrew, vol. 1

[ ] Hebrew compared with Paleo-Greek, vol. 2

[ ] Hebrew compared with Greek, vol. 3

[ ] Hebrew compared with Aramaic, vol. 4

[ ] Combined Level 1-4 Hebrew Comparisons

LEVELS 1-4
Greek Comparisons

[ ] Greek compared with Paleo-Hebrew, vol. 1

[ ] Greek compared with Paleo-Greek, vol. 2

[ ] Greek compared with Hebrew, vol. 3

[ ] Greek compared with Aramaic, vol. 4

[ ] Combined Level 1-4 Greek Comparisons

LEVELS 1-4
Aramaic Comparisons

[ ] Aramaic compared with Paleo-Hebrew, vol. 1

[ ] Aramaic compared with Paleo-Greek, vol. 2

[ ] Aramaic compared with Hebrew, vol. 3

[ ] Aramaic compared with Greek, vol. 4

[ ] Combined Level 1-4 Aramaic Comparisons

ALPHABETS

LEVELS 1-5
Paleo-Hebrew Comparisons

[ ] Paleo-Hebrew compared with Paleo-Greek, vol. 1

[ ] Paleo-Hebrew compared with Hebrew, vol. 2

[ ] Paleo-Hebrew compared with Greek, vol. 3

[ ] Paleo-Hebrew compared with Aramaic, vol. 4

[ ] Combined Levels 1-5 Paleo-Hebrew Comparisons

LEVELS 1-5
Paleo-Greek Comparisons

[ ] Paleo-Greek compared with Paleo-Hebrew, vol. 1

[ ] Paleo-Greek compared with Hebrew, vol. 2

[ ] Paleo-Greek compared with Greek, vol. 3

[ ] Paleo-Greek compared with Aramaic, vol. 4

[ ] Combined Levels 1-5 Paleo-Greek Comparisons

LEVELS 1-5
Hebrew Comparisons

[ ] Hebrew compared with Paleo-Hebrew, vol. 1

[ ] Hebrew compared with Paleo-Greek, vol. 2

[ ] Hebrew compared with Greek, vol. 3

[ ] Hebrew compared with Aramaic, vol. 4

[ ] Hebrew compared with Proto Sinaitic, vol. 5

[ ] Combined Levels 1-5 Hebrew Comparisons

LEVELS 1-5
Greek Comparisons

[ ] Greek compared with Paleo-Hebrew, vol. 1

[ ] Greek compared with Paleo-Greek, vol. 2

[ ] Greek compared with Hebrew, vol. 3

[ ] Greek compared with Aramaic, vol. 4

[ ] Combined Levels 1-5 Greek Comparisons

LEVELS 1-5
Aramaic Comparisons

[ ] Aramaic compared with Paleo-Hebrew, vol. 1

[ ] Aramaic compared with Paleo-Greek, vol. 2

[ ] Aramaic compared with Hebrew, vol. 3

[ ] Aramaic compared with Greek, vol. 4

[ ] Combined Levels 1-5 Aramaic Comparisons

ALPHABETS

LEVELS 1-6
Paleo-Hebrew Comparisons

[ ] Paleo-Hebrew compared with Paleo-Greek, vol. 1

[ ] Paleo-Hebrew compared with Hebrew, vol. 2

[ ] Paleo-Hebrew compared with Greek, vol. 3

[ ] Paleo-Hebrew compared with Aramaic, vol. 4

[ ] Combined Levels 1-6 Paleo-Hebrew Comparisons

LEVELS 1-6
Paleo-Greek Comparisons

[ ] Paleo-Greek compared with Paleo-Hebrew, vol. 1

[ ] Paleo-Greek compared with Hebrew, vol. 2

[ ] Paleo-Greek compared with Greek, vol. 3

[ ] Paleo-Greek compared with Aramaic, vol. 4

[ ] Combined Levels 1-6 Paleo-Greek Comparisons

LEVELS 1-6
Hebrew Comparisons

[ ] Hebrew compared with Paleo-Hebrew, vol. 1

[ ] Hebrew compared with Paleo-Greek, vol. 2

[ ] Hebrew compared with Greek, vol. 3

[ ] Hebrew compared with Aramaic, vol. 4

[ ] Combined Levels 1-6 Hebrew Comparisons

LEVELS 1-6
Greek Comparisons

[ ] Greek compared with Paleo-Hebrew, vol. 1

[ ] Greek compared with Paleo-Greek, vol. 2

[ ] Greek compared with Hebrew, vol. 3

[ ] Greek compared with Aramaic, vol. 4

[ ] Combined Levels 1-6 Greek Comparisons

LEVELS 1-6
Aramaic Egyptian Hieroglyphic Match Comparisons

[ ] Aramaic compared with Paleo-Hebrew, vol. 1

[ ] Aramaic compared with Paleo-Greek, vol. 2

[ ] Aramaic compared with Hebrew, vol. 3

[ ] Aramaic compared with Greek, vol. 4

[ ] Combined Levels 1-6 Aramaic Comparisons

ALPHABETS
LEVELS 1-7
Paleo-Hebrew Comparisons

[ ] Paleo-Hebrew compared with Paleo-Greek, vol. 1

[ ] Paleo-Hebrew compared with Hebrew, vol. 2

[ ] Paleo-Hebrew compared with Greek, vol. 3

[ ] Paleo-Hebrew compared with Aramaic, vol. 4

[ ] Paleo-Hebrew compared with Proto Sinaitic, vol. 5

[ ] Combined Levels 1- 7 Paleo-Hebrew Comparisons

LEVELS 1-7
Paleo-Greek Comparisons

[ ] Paleo-Greek compared with Paleo-Hebrew, vol. 1

[ ] Paleo-Greek compared with Hebrew, vol. 2

[ ] Paleo-Greek compared with Greek, vol. 3

[ ] Paleo-Greek compared with Aramaic, vol. 4

[ ] Paleo-Greek compared with Proto Sinaitic, vol. 5

[ ] Combined Levels 1- 7 Paleo-Greek Comparisons

LEVELS 1-7
Hebrew Comparisons

[ ] Hebrew compared with Paleo-Hebrew, vol. 1

[ ] Hebrew compared with Paleo-Greek, vol. 2

[ ] Hebrew compared with Greek, vol. 3

[ ] Hebrew compared with Aramaic, vol. 4

[ ] Hebrew compared with Proto Sinaitic, vol. 5

[ ] Combined Levels 1- 7 Hebrew Comparisons

LEVELS 1-7
Greek Comparisons

[ ] Greek compared with Paleo-Hebrew, vol. 1

[ ] Greek compared with Paleo-Greek, vol. 2

[ ] Greek compared with Hebrew, vol. 3

[ ] Greek compared with Aramaic, vol. 4

[ ] Greek compared with Proto Sinaitic, vol. 5

[ ] Combined Levels 1- 7 Greek Comparisons

LEVELS 1-7
Aramaic Comparisons

[ ] Aramaic compared with Paleo-Hebrew, vol. 1

[ ] Aramaic compared with Paleo-Greek, vol. 2

[ ] Aramaic compared with Hebrew, vol. 3

[ ] Aramaic compared with Greek, vol. 4

[ ] Aramaic compared with Proto Sinaitic, vol. 5

[ ] Combined Levels 1-7 Aramaic Comparisons

LEVELS 1-7
Proto Sinaitic Comparisons

[ ] Proto Sinaitic compared with Paleo-Hebrew, vol. 1

[ ] Proto Sinaitic compared with Paleo-Greek, vol. 2

[ ] Proto Sinaitic compared with Hebrew, vol. 3

[ ] Proto Sinaitic compared with Greek, vol. 4

[ ] Proto Sinaitic compared with Aramaic, vol. 5

[ ] Combined levels 1-7 Proto Sinaitic Comparisons

ALPHABETS
LEVELS 2-3
Paleo-Hebrew Comparisons

[ ] Paleo-Greek compared with Paleo-Hebrew, vol. 1

[ ] Hebrew compared with Paleo-Hebrew, vol. 2

[ ] Greek compared with Paleo-Hebrew, vol. 3

[ ] Aramaic compared with Paleo-Hebrew, vol. 4

[ ] Proto Sinaitic compared with Paleo-Hebrew, vol. 5

[ ] Combined Levels 2-3 Paleo-Hebrew Comparisons

LEVELS 2-3
Paleo-Greek Comparisons

[ ] Paleo-Hebrew compared with Paleo-Greek, vol. 1

[ ] Hebrew compared with Paleo-Greek, vol. 2

[ ] Greek compared with Paleo-Greek, vol. 3

[ ] Aramaic compared with Paleo-Greek, vol. 4

[ ] Proto Sinaitic compared with Paleo-Greek, vol. 5

[ ] Combined Levels 2-3 Paleo-Greek Comparisons

LEVELS 2-3
Hebrew Comparisons

[ ] Paleo-Hebrew compared with Hebrew, vol. 1

[ ] Paleo-Greek compared with Hebrew, vol. 2

[ ] Greek compared with Hebrew, vol. 3

[ ] Aramaic compared with Hebrew, vol. 4

[ ] Proto Sinaitic compared with Hebrew, vol. 5

[ ] Combined Levels 2-3 Hebrew Comparisons

LEVELS 2-3
Greek Comparisons

[ ] Paleo-Hebrew compared with Greek, vol. 1

[ ] Paleo-Greek compared with Greek, vol. 2

[ ] Hebrew compared with Greek, vol. 3

[ ] Aramaic compared with Greek, vol. 4

[ ] Proto Sinaitic compared with Greek, vol. 5

[ ] Combined Levels 2-3 Greek Comparisons

LEVELS 2-3
Aramaic Comparisons

[ ] Paleo-Hebrew letters compared with Aramaic, vol. 1

[ ] Paleo-Greek letters compared with Aramaic, vol. 2

[ ] Hebrew letters compared with Aramaic, vol. 3

[ ] Greek letters compared with Aramaic, vol. 4

[ ] Proto Sinaitic letters compared with Aramaic, vol. 5

[ ] Combined Levels 2-3 Aramaic Comparisons

LEVELS 2-3
Proto Sinaitic Comparisons

[ ] Paleo-Hebrew compared with Proto Sinaitic, vol. 1

[ ] Paleo-Greek compared with Proto Sinaitic, vol. 2

[ ] Hebrew compared with Proto Sinaitic, vol. 3

[ ] Greek compared with Proto Sinaitic, vol. 4

[ ] Aramaic compared with Proto Sinaitic, vol. 5

[ ] Combined Levels 2-3 Proto Sinaitic Comparisons

ALPHABETS

LEVELS 1-4
Paleo-Hebrew Comparisons

[ ] Paleo-Greek compared with Paleo-Hebrew, vol. 1

[ ] Hebrew compared with Paleo-Hebrew, vol. 2

[ ] Greek compared with Paleo-Hebrew, vol. 3

[ ] Aramaic compared with Paleo-Hebrew, vol. 4

[ ] Combined Levels 1-4 Paleo-Hebrew Comparisons

LEVELS 1-4
Paleo-Greek Comparisons

[ ] Paleo-Hebrew compared with Paleo-Greek, vol. 1

[ ] Hebrew compared with Paleo-Greek, vol. 2

[ ] Greek compared with Paleo-Greek, vol. 3

[ ] Aramaic compared with Paleo-Greek, vol. 4

[ ] Combined Levels 1-4 Paleo-Greek Comparisons

LEVELS 1-4
Hebrew Comparisons

[ ] Paleo-Hebrew compared with Hebrew, vol. 1

[ ] Paleo-Greek compared with Hebrew, vol. 2

[ ] Greek compared with Hebrew, vol. 3

[ ] Aramaic compared with Hebrew, vol. 4

[ ] Combined Levels 1-4 Hebrew Comparisons

LEVELS 1-4
Greek Comparisons

[ ] Paleo-Hebrew names compared with Greek, vol. 1

[ ] Paleo-Greek names compared with Greek, vol. 2

[ ] Hebrew names compared with Greek, vol. 3

[ ] Aramaic names compared with Greek, vol. 4

[ ] Combined Levels 1-4 Greek Comparisons

LEVELS 1-4
Aramaic Comparisons

[ ] Paleo-Hebrew compared with Aramaic, vol. 1

[ ] Paleo-Greek compared with Aramaic, vol. 2

[ ] Hebrew compared with Aramaic, vol. 3

[ ] Greek compared with Aramaic, vol. 4

[ ] Combined Levels 1-4 Aramaic Comparisons

ALPHABETS

LEVELS 1-5
Paleo-Hebrew Comparisons

[ ] Paleo-Greek compared with Paleo-Hebrew, vol. 1

[ ] Hebrew compared with Paleo-Hebrew, vol. 2

[ ] Greek compared with Paleo-Hebrew, vol. 3

[ ] Aramaic compared with Paleo-Hebrew, vol. 4

[ ] Combined Levels 1-5 Paleo-Hebrew Comparisons

LEVELS 1-5
Paleo-Greek Comparisons

[ ] Paleo-Hebrew compared with Paleo-Greek, vol. 1

[ ] Hebrew compared with Paleo-Greek, vol. 2

[ ] Greek compared with Paleo-Greek, vol. 3

[ ] Aramaic compared with Paleo-Greek, vol. 4

[ ] Combined Levels 1-5 Paleo-Greek Comparisons

LEVELS 1-5
Hebrew Comparisons

[ ] Paleo-Hebrew compared with Hebrew, vol. 1

[ ] Paleo-Greek compared with Hebrew, vol. 2

[ ] Greek compared with Hebrew, vol. 3

[ ] Aramaic compared with Hebrew, vol. 4

[ ] Combined Levels 1-5 Hebrew Comparisons

LEVELS 1-5
Greek Comparisons

[ ] Paleo-Hebrew compared with Greek, vol. 1

[ ] Paleo-Greek compared with Greek, vol. 2

[ ] Hebrew compared with Greek, vol. 3

[ ] Aramaic compared with Greek, vol. 4

[ ] Combined Levels 1-5 Greek Comparisons

LEVELS 1-5
Aramaic Comparisons

[ ] Paleo-Hebrew compared with Aramaic, vol. 1

[ ] Paleo-Greek compared with Aramaic, vol. 2

[ ] Hebrew compared with Aramaic, vol. 3

[ ] Greek compared with Aramaic, vol. 4

[ ] Combined Levels 1-5 Aramaic Comparisons

ALPHABETS
LEVELS 1-6
Paleo-Hebrew Comparisons

[ ] Paleo-Greek compared with Paleo-Hebrew, vol. 1

[ ] Hebrew compared with Paleo-Hebrew, vol. 2

[ ] Greek compared with Paleo-Hebrew, vol. 3

[ ] Aramaic compared with Paleo-Hebrew, vol. 4

[ ] Combined Levels 1-6 Paleo-Hebrew Comparisons

LEVELS 1-6
Paleo-Greek Comparisons

[ ] Paleo-Hebrew compared with Paleo-Greek, vol. 1

[ ] Hebrew compared with Paleo-Greek, vol. 2

[ ] Greek compared with Paleo-Greek, vol. 3

[ ] Aramaic compared with Paleo-Greek, vol. 4

[ ] Combined Levels 1-6 Paleo-Greek Comparisons

LEVELS 1-6
Hebrew Comparisons

[ ] Paleo-Hebrew compared with Hebrew, vol. 1

[ ] Paleo-Greek compared with Hebrew, vol. 2

[ ] Greek compared with Hebrew, vol. 3

[ ] Aramaic compared with Hebrew, vol. 4

[ ] Combined Levels 1-6 Hebrew Comparisons

LEVELS 1-6
Greek Comparisons

[ ] Paleo-Hebrew compared with Greek, vol. 1

[ ] Paleo-Greek compared with Greek, vol. 2

[ ] Hebrew compared with Greek, vol. 3

[ ] Aramaic compared with Greek, vol. 4

[ ] Combined Levels 1-6 Greek Comparisons

LEVELS 1-6
Aramaic Comparisons

[ ] Paleo-Hebrew compared with Aramaic, vol. 1

[ ] Paleo-Greek compared with Aramaic, vol. 2

[ ] Hebrew compared with Aramaic, vol. 3

[ ] Greek compared with Aramaic, vol. 4

[ ] Combined Levels 1-6 Aramaic Comparisons

ALPHABETS
LEVELS 1-7
Paleo-Hebrew Comparisons

[ ] Paleo-Greek compared with Paleo-Hebrew, vol. 1

[ ] Hebrew compared with Paleo-Hebrew, vol. 2

[ ] Greek compared with Paleo-Hebrew, vol. 3

[ ] Aramaic compared with Paleo-Hebrew, vol. 4

[ ] Proto Sinaitic compared with Paleo-Hebrew, vol. 5

[ ] Combined Level 1-7 Paleo-Hebrew Comparisons

LEVELS 1-7
Paleo-Greek Comparisons

[ ] Paleo-Hebrew compared with Paleo-Greek, vol. 1

[ ] Hebrew compared with Paleo-Greek, vol. 2

[ ] Greek compared with Paleo-Greek, vol. 3

[ ] Aramaic compared with Paleo-Greek, vol. 4

[ ] Proto Sinaitic compared with Paleo-Greek, vol. 5

[ ] Combined Level 1-7 Paleo-Greek Comparisons

LEVELS 1-7
Hebrew Comparisons

[ ] Paleo-Hebrew compared with Hebrew, vol. 1

[ ] Paleo-Greek compared with Hebrew, vol. 2

[ ] Greek compared with Hebrew, vol. 3

[ ] Aramaic compared with Hebrew, vol. 4

[ ] Proto Sinaitic compared with Hebrew, vol. 5

[ ] Combined Level 1-7 Hebrew Comparisons

LEVELS 1-7
Greek Comparisons

[ ] Paleo-Hebrew compared with Greek, vol. 1

[ ] Paleo-Greek compared with Greek, vol. 2

[ ] Hebrew compared with Greek, vol. 3

[ ] Aramaic compared with Greek, vol. 4

[ ] Proto Sinaitic compared with Greek, vol. 5

[ ] Combined Level 1-7 Greek Comparisons

LEVELS 1-7
Aramaic Comparisons

[ ] Paleo-Hebrew compared with Aramaic, vol. 1

[ ] Paleo-Greek compared with Aramaic, vol. 2

[ ] Hebrew compared with Aramaic, vol. 3

[ ] Greek compared with Aramaic, vol. 4

[ ] Proto Sinaitic compared with Aramaic, vol. 5

[ ] Combined Level 1-7 Aramaic Comparisons

LEVELS 1-7
Proto Sinaitic Comparisons

[ ] Paleo-Hebrew compared with Proto Sinaitic, vol. 1

[ ] Paleo-Greek compared with Proto Sinaitic, vol. 2

[ ] Hebrew compared with Proto Sinaitic, vol. 3

[ ] Greek compared with Proto Sinaitic, vol. 4

[ ] Aramaic compared with Proto Sinaitic, vol. 5

[ ] Combined level 1-7 Proto Sinaitic Comparisons

Other books by
Travis Wayne Goodsell

An Introduction to Paleo-Hebrew Alphabet and
  Grammar A New Theory
Translating the Book of Abraham
Answers to Still Asked Gospel Questions
Devoted to Studying the Scriptures: A Scripture
  Study Manual
Idolatry
Joseph Smith as a Translator: Fireside Series
Joseph Smith as Ancient Translator: A Scribe's
    Viewpoint
Ancient Language 101 Lesson Manuals
    Paleo-Hebrew 101 Lesson Manual, Vol. 1
    Paleo-Greek 101 Lesson Manual, Vol. 2
    Hebrew 101 Lesson Manual, Vol. 3
    Greek 101 Lesson Manual, Vol. 4
Philosophy of Mormonism
The Origins of the Alphabet Series
    The Origins of the Paleo-Hebrew Alphabet
        A New Theory
    The Origins of the Hebrew Alphabet A
        New Theory
    The Origins of the Paleo-Greek Alphabet A
        New Theory
    The Origins of the Greek Alphabet A New
        Theory 2nd Edition
University Papers
Modern American Utopia
Modern American Utopia part 2: The Republic
BDB Reconstructed Dictionary
Paleo-Hebrew Vocabulary Theory Test Series
    Three-Letter Hebrew Vocabulary Test
    Complete Hebrew Vocabulary Theory Test
    Third Letter Prefix Determinative
        Vocabulary Theory Test

Level 1 Ancient Alphabets series
  Level 1 Ancient Alphabet: Paleo-Hebrew Letters, vol. 1
  Level 1 Ancient Alphabet Paleo-Greek Letters, vol. 2
  Level 1 Ancient Alphabet Hebrew Letters, vol. 3
  Level 1 Ancient Alphabet Greek Letters, vol. 4
  Level 1 Ancient Alphabet Aramaic Letters, vol. 5
  Level 1 Ancient Alphabet Proto Sinaitic Letters, vol. 6
Ancient Alphabets Combined Level series
  Level 1 Ancient Alphabet Letters, Vol. 1
Level 2 Ancient Alphabets series
  Level 2 Ancient Alphabet: Paleo-Hebrew Names, vol. 1
  Level 2 Ancient Alphabet: Paleo-Greek Names, vol. 2
  Level 2 Ancient Alphabet: Hebrew Names, vol. 3
  Level 2 Ancient Alphabet: Greek Names, vol. 4
  Level 2 Ancient Alphabet: Aramaic Names, vol. 5
  Level 2 Ancient Alphabet: Proto Sinaitic Names, vol. 6
Ancient Alphabets Combined Level series
  Level 2 Ancient Alphabet Names, Vol. 2
Level 3 Ancient Alphabets series
  Level 3 Ancient Alphabet: Paleo-Hebrew Phonemes, vol. 1
  Level 3 Ancient Alphabet: Paleo-Greek Phonemes, vol. 2
  Level 3 Ancient Alphabet: Hebrew Phonemes, vol. 3
  Level 3 Ancient Alphabet: Greek Phonemes, vol. 4
  Level 3 Ancient Alphabet: Aramaic Phonemes, vol. 5
  Level 3 Ancient Alphabet: Proto Sinaitic Phonemes, vol. 6
Ancient Alphabets Combined Level Series
  Level 3 Ancient Alphabet Phonemes Vol. 3
Level 4 Ancient Alphabets series
  Level 4 Ancient Alphabet: Paleo-Hebrew Egyptian Hieroglyphic
    Matches, vol. 1
  Level 4 Ancient Alphabet: Paleo-Greek Egyptian Hieroglyphic
    Matches, vol. 2
  Level 4 Ancient Alphabet: Hebrew Egyptian Hieroglyphic Matches, vol. 3
  Level 4 Ancient Alphabet: Greek Egyptian Hieroglyphic Matches, vol. 4
  Level 4 Ancient Alphabet: Aramaic Egyptian Hieroglyphic Matches, vol. 5
Ancient Alphabets Combined Level Series
  Level 4 Ancient Alphabet Egyptian Hieroglyphic Matches, vol. 4

YouTube Videos

http://www.youtube.com/c/TravisWayneGoodsell1970

Updated Paleo-Hebrew Alphabet A New Theory

An Introduction to Paleo-Hebrew Alphabet and Grammar A New Theory

Restoring the Torah the Creation Story Genesis ch 1 v1

Restoring the Torah Genesis 1:2

Restoring the Torah Genesis 1v3

Philsophy of Mormonism Good and Evil

Restoring the Tanakh Amos 3:7

Stem Rod Root

Book of Abraham facsimile #1

Book of Abraham facsimile #2

Book of Abraham facsimile #3

Restoring the Greek Alphabet

Restoring the Aramaic Alphabet

Philosophy of Mormonism The Spirit

Prophesy of Osiris

Restoring the Torah the Paleo-Hebrew Alphabet A New Theory

Restoring the Torah the Paleo-Hebrew Vocabulary A New Theory

Restoring the Torah part 1

Websites

www.travis-wayne-goodsell.weebly.com

www.paleohebrewegyptian.weebly.com

www.joseph-smith-as-ancient-translator.weebly.com

www.mormon-philosophy.weebly.com

www.lds-interpretationsofdreams.weebly.com

www.utopia-oftravis-wayne-goodsell.weebly.com

www.goodsells-lds-commentaries-and-manuals.weebly.com

www.book-of-abraham-graphers.weebly.com

Contributing Websites

www.mographers.weebly.com

www.book-of-mormon-mographers.weebly.com

www.book-of-abraham-mographers.weebly.com

www.old-testament-mographers.weebly.com

www.new-testament.mographers.weebly.com

www.doctrine-and-covenants-mographers.weebly.com

www.book-of-joseph-mographers.weebly.com

www.egyptian-alphabet-and-grammar-mographers.weebly.com

www.egyptian-mographers.weebly.com

Author Pages

http://www.amazon.com/Travis-Wayne-Goodsell/e/B00Z7HYKM0/ref=sr_tc_2_0?qid=1450547544&sr=1-2-ent

www.google.com/+TravisWayneGoodsell1970

http://outskirtspress.com/paleohebrewalphabetandgrammar

About the Author, Travis Wayne Goodsell

Travis is an Abecedarian, Lexicographer, and Translator (taking a written foreign language and turning it into English) of ancient languages. He is a graduate of the University of Lethbridge, in Alberta, Canada. He majored in Biblical Studies, studying under Thomas Robinson, and Philosophy of Science, the field of scientific research theory. He minored in ancient languages, disciplining in Biblical Hebrew under W. E. Aufrecht, who studied under Professor Thomas O. Lambin of Harvard University; Greek under Thomas Robinson, and Latin. He also attended the University of Utah, disciplining in Egyptology under Ewa Wasilewska.